CIVIL WAR CHRONICLES

LEE VERSUS GRANT

GREAT BATTLES OF THE CIVIL WAR

By Ruth Ashby

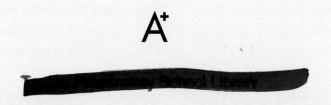

For Ernie   —R.A.

Published by Smart Apple Media
1980 Lookout Drive, North Mankato, Minnesota 56003

Produced by Byron Preiss Visual Publications, Inc.

Library of Congress Cataloging-in-Publication Data
Ashby, Ruth.
Lee v. Grant: Great Battles of the Civil War / by Ruth Ashby
v. cm. — (Civil War chronicles)
Contents: Introduction: the surrender at Appomattox — Grant's background —
Lee's background — Grant in battle: Fort Donelson, Shiloh, Vicksburg, Chattanooga
— Lee in battle: Peninsular campaign, Seven Days' Battles, Antietam,
Chancellorsville, Gettysburg — Grant v. Lee: The Wilderness, Cold Harbor,
Petersburg, Appomattox Courthouse and the end of the war —Lee and Grant after
the war.
ISBN 1-58340-184-9
1. United States—History—Civil War, 1861-1865—Campaigns—Juvenile literature.
2. Lee, Robert E. (Robert Edward), 1807-1870—Juvenile literature. 3. Grant, Ulysses
S. (Ulysses Simpson), 1822-1885—Juvenile literature. [1. United States—History—
Civil War, 1861-1865—Campaigns. 2. Lee, Robert E. (Robert Edward), 1807-1870. 3.
Grant, Ulysses S. (Ulysses Simpson), 1822-1885. 4. Generals.] I. Title: Lee versus
Grant. II. Title.

E470 .A84 2002
973.7'3—dc21   2002017645

First Edition
9 8 7 6 5 4 3 2 1

Contents

Introduction

The Civil War was the great American tragedy. From 1861 to 1865, it divided states, broke up families, took the lives of more than half a million people, and left much of the country in ruins. But it also abolished the great national shame of slavery and cleared the way for the astounding expansion of American industry and culture in the second half of the 19th century. Without the war, the United States would not have been so progressive or so united—and millions of its people would still have been in chains. In the end it was, perhaps, a necessary tragedy.

The conflict had loomed for decades. From the Constitutional Convention in 1787 on, the North and South disagreed about whether slavery should exist in the United States. In the North, slavery was gradually abolished between 1780 and 1827. But the South became ever more yoked to slavery as its economy became more dependent on the production of cotton. In the meantime, the United States was expanding westward. Every time a territory became a new state, the government had to decide whether it would be slave or free. For 40 years, Congress reached compromise after compromise.

Finally, differences could no longer be bandaged over. With the election of Republican Abraham Lincoln to the presidency in 1860, a crisis was reached. Southern states were afraid that Lincoln, who opposed slavery in the territories, would try to abolish it in the South as well—and that their economy and way of life would be destroyed. On December 20, 1860, South Carolina seceded from the Union. It was

✉ Abraham Lincoln

✉ Jefferson Davis

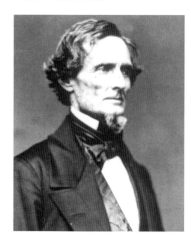

Robert E. Lee ⊠

Ulysses S. Grant ⊠

followed by Alabama, Florida, Georgia, Louisiana, Mississippi, Texas, Virginia, North Carolina, Tennessee, and Arkansas.

The rebellious states formed a new nation, the Confederate States of America, and elected a president, Jefferson Davis. On April 12, 1861, Confederate forces fired on the Federal post of Fort Sumter in Charleston Harbor—and the Civil War began. It lasted four years and touched the lives of every man, woman, and child in the nation. There were heroes on both sides, in the army and on the home front, from Union general Ulysses S. Grant and Confederate general Robert E. Lee to black leader Harriet Tubman and poet and nurse Walt Whitman. It is estimated that at least 620,000 soldiers were killed, almost as many Americans as in all other armed conflicts combined. When Lincoln issued the Emancipation Proclamation on January 1, 1863, and freed the slaves in the rebellious states, it became not just a war for reunification but a war of liberation as well.

Lee versus Grant portrays the desperate duel of the two major military figures of the war—Ulysses S. Grant, the Union general whose masterful strategy won the war for the North, and Robert E. Lee, the Confederate commander whose brilliant tactics and inspired leadership won him the admiration of both the North and the South.

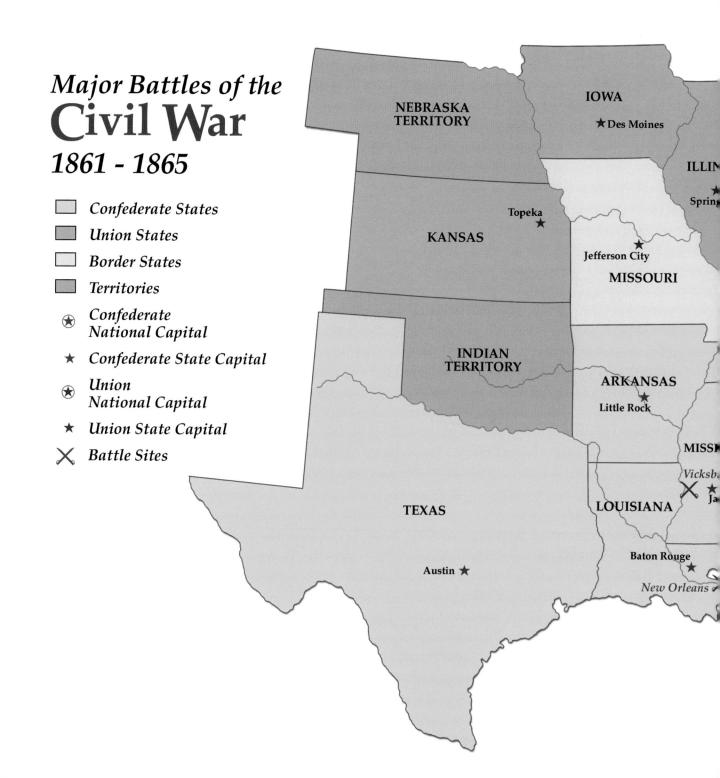

Major Battles of the
Civil War
1861 - 1865

	Confederate States
	Union States
	Border States
	Territories
✪	Confederate National Capital
★	Confederate State Capital
✪	Union National Capital
★	Union State Capital
✕	Battle Sites

NEBRASKA TERRITORY

IOWA
★Des Moines

ILLIN
★
Spring

Topeka
★

KANSAS

★
Jefferson City

MISSOURI

INDIAN
TERRITORY

ARKANSAS
★
Little Rock

MISS

Vicksb
✕ ★
Ja

TEXAS

LOUISIANA

Baton Rouge
★

Austin ★

New Orleans

BATTLES (on map below)

1 *Gettysburg*
2 *Antietam*
3 *Shenandoah Campaign*
4 *First and Second Manassas*
5 *Wilderness*
6 *Fredericksburg*
7 *Spotsylvania*
8 *Chancellorsville*
9 *Cold Harbor*
10 *Seven Days' Battles*
11 *Petersburg*
12 *Peninsular Campaign*
13 *First and Second Hampton Roads*

INDIANA
★ Indianapolis

OHIO
★ Columbus

PENNSYLVANIA
★ Harrisburg

NEW JERSEY
★ Trenton

Gettysburg ✕
Antietam ✕

WEST VIRGINIA
★ Charleston

Annapolis ★
★ Dover
DELAWARE

Washington, D.C. ⊛

MARYLAND

★ Frankfort

KENTUCKY

VIRGINIA
(enlarged below)

⊛ Richmond

Fort Donelson ✕

TENNESSEE
★ Nashville

NORTH CAROLINA
★ Raleigh

Chattanooga ✕
✕ *Shiloh*
Chickamauga ✕

★ Columbia

SOUTH CAROLINA

✕ *Atlanta*

ALABAMA

★ Milledgeville

★ Montgomery

GEORGIA

Fort Sumter ✕

✕ *Savannah*

★ Tallahassee

✕ *Mobile Bay*

FLORIDA

Inset map

PENNSYLVANIA

MARYLAND

WEST VIRGINIA
*admitted to the Union
June 20, 1863*

Washington, D.C. ⊛

★ Annapolis

1

3

4

5 6
8 7

VIRGINIA

Richmond ⊛ 9
10

Appomattox •

11

12

13

✠ Ulysses S. Grant and Robert E. Lee in a romanticized portrait done after the Civil War.
Even though they fought on different sides, both men are remembered as American heroes.

Chapter One

Appomattox

It was the afternoon of April 9, 1865. Confederate commander Robert E. Lee was waiting for Union general Ulysses S. Grant in Wilmer McLean's parlor in Appomattox Court House, Virginia. Lee had dressed with particular care when he awoke at 3:00 that morning, in a new gray uniform, dashing red sash, and shiny black knee-high boots. Around his waist he buckled his dress sword, which had a gold-embroidered scabbard. That morning, at dawn, his Army of Northern Virginia had made a last-attempt assault upon Union troops. The charge had not lasted long. The 23,000 Confederates, worn and starving, had found themselves surrounded by 80,000 Union soldiers. Lee had realized the end had come. "There is nothing left for me to do but to go and see General Grant," Lee had said sadly. "And I would rather die a thousand deaths."

The Wilmer McLean House, where General Robert E. Lee surrendered the Army of Northern Virginia.

Half an hour after Lee had arrived, Grant strode into the parlor chewing on a half-smoked cigar. That day he had dressed for battle in stained, mud-spattered boots and an ordinary private's shirt. "I must have contrasted very strangely," Grant admitted later, "with a man so handsomely dressed, six feet [183 cm] high, and of faultless form."

The two men shook hands and sat down at a small table. There, after four years of heroic, brutal, and at last hopeless fighting, the Virginia aristocrat surrendered his army to the son of an Ohio tanner.

The two commanders seemed as different as they could be. Yet two more brave, brilliant, and decent men could not be found in their now-reunited nation.

Young Grant

Hiram Ulysses Grant was born in Point Pleasant, Ohio, on April 27, 1822, the son of Jesse R. Grant and Hannah Simpson Grant. The energetic and talkative Jesse opened a tannery in Georgetown, Ohio, where Ulysses, as Hiram was called, grew up. Like many sons of aggressively outgoing fathers, Ulysses was quiet and reserved. He always disliked his father's business, with its bloody hides and disgusting smells. Even as an adult he could eat meat only if it was charred black because he hated the sight of blood so much. It was a strange beginning for a boy who would someday be a soldier.

From the first, Ulysses had a gift for handling horses. As his mother said, "Horses seem to understand Ulysses." By the time he was 8, he was already hauling all the wood for the tannery, and when he was 10, he had his own freight and passenger business. Although Ulysses was a small, sensitive-looking child, with red hair and blue-gray eyes, his father knew that he could take care of himself. Already the boy carried himself with a calm self-confidence.

The schoolhouse in Georgetown, Ohio, that Grant attended when he was a boy.

One childhood incident seemed to foreshadow Grant's future economic difficulties. His father gave him permission to buy his own colt from a man named Ralston. When Ralston asked Ulysses how much his father had said he should offer, the boy blurted out the truth: He should offer $20, but could go up to $25 if necessary. Needless to say, he ended up paying the full

amount for the colt. It was not the first time he would demonstrate his business naïveté.

Ironically, mathematics was Grant's best subject in school. His self-educated father wanted his sons to have a good education, and he obtained an appointment to the West Point Military Academy for Ulysses. Ulysses was not a standout at West Point; his natural sloppiness and academic mediocrity earned him many demerits. When he graduated in 1843, he ranked 21 in a class of 39. Grant did not intend to remain in the military. Eventually he thought he might try to be a mathematics professor.

But first he had a mandatory tour of duty. Two years after he was assigned to the Fourth U.S. Infantry, his regiment was dispatched to fight in the Mexican War. Like the future president Abraham Lincoln, Grant was totally opposed to the war. It was "one of the most unjust [actions] ever waged by a stronger against a weaker nation . . . to acquire additional territory," he wrote later. But he would do his duty despite his personal opinion. Grant proved again and again to be calm and level-headed in the heat of battle. Once, on a mission to get ammunition for his troops, he rode boldly through enemy fire, clinging to one side of his horse as it galloped through the streets of Monterrey. Another time, he led a group of men to drag cannons up the belfry of a church to bomb Mexico City. For his daring action, Grant was promoted to captain.

In 1848, with the war won, Grant finally had time to marry his sweetheart, Julia Dent, a lively woman who loved horses almost as much as Grant did. They would be married 37 years and have four children. As devoted to his Julia as she was to him, Grant would insist that she accompany him on many of his Civil War campaigns.

At this point in his career, however, Grant had to go back alone to a frontier post at Fort Vancouver. Lonely and bored, he began to drink

Ulysses S. Grant at the Battle of Mexico City. During the battle, he had his men carry artillery up a church belfry. He turned a cannon on a city gate and drove the defenders away.

too much. He also invested in a series of failed business ventures. "You do not know how forsaken I feel here," Grant wrote to Julia. "Sometimes I get so anxious to see you and our little boys, that I am almost tempted to resign and trust to Providence." Soon he did not have a choice. His heavy drinking forced him to resign. Grant returned to Julia's father's farm in St. Louis as a civilian.

During the next four years, Grant tried his hand at farming, real estate, and working in a customhouse. Through bad luck and bad judgment, all his undertakings failed. Finally, at age 37, Grant was forced to take hat in hand and ask his father for a job in his leather goods store in Galena, Illinois. It turned out that he was not even a very good sales clerk. It looked as if Grant was doomed to be a failure. But then came the Civil War.

Young Lee

Born on January 19, 1807, Robert Edward Lee was 15 years older than Ulysses S. Grant. Robert was a Lee of Virginia, the son of Henry Lee, also known as "Light Horse Harry," who had served brilliantly under George Washington in the Revolutionary War. But by the time Robert was born, his father was bankrupt and in disgrace. Harry Lee abandoned his family when Robert was only five and sailed off to the West Indies, where he died a few years later.

Robert was raised by his mother, Anne Hill Carter Lee, in Alexandria, Virginia, and educated at her family's school. (The Carters were so rich and so numerous that they had their own private schools for boys and girls.) Robert was a good-tempered, diligent child who excelled at sports and horsemanship. Keenly aware of his father's disgrace, he grew up determined to restore the good family name. He was also a

Quick Facts

★ Wilmer McLean used to say that the Civil War started in his front yard and ended in his parlor. Artillery fire struck his home on the battlefield during the First Battle of Bull Run in 1861. Leaving northern Virginia for a safer neighborhood, he moved south to Appomattox Courthouse. There, four years later, McLean hosted the surrender of Lee to Grant.

★ The "S" in Ulysses S. Grant's name and the omission of his real first name, Hiram, came from a clerical error when he received his appointment to West Point. He used to say it stood for Simpson, his mother's maiden name.

★ Most of the generals who fought in the Civil War gained battle experience in the Mexican War. This was where both Grant and Lee had a chance to assess the abilities of the men who would be either their comrades or their enemies: Confederates James Longstreet, George Pickett, Thomas J. "Stonewall" Jackson, and Joseph Johnston, and Federals George Gordon Meade, George B. McClellan, and Joseph Hooker.

★ Grant and Lee met briefly during the Mexican War. Grant would later remember the encounter; Lee would not.

devoted son to his mother, whose health worsened throughout his child-hood. By the time he was 11, he ran the household himself, doing the shopping, balancing the budget, and caring for his mother.

Anne Lee knew she would soon have to let her beloved son go. A military education seemed like a good idea for a boy who idolized George Washington. Through family contacts, Robert obtained a coveted spot at West Point. He proved to be a model cadet. "He was a most exemplary pupil in every respect," a teacher wrote later. "He was never behind time at his studies; never failed in a single recitation; was perfectly observant of the rules and regulations of the institution; was gentlemanly, unobstructive, and respectful in all his deportment to teachers and his fellow students." Lee went on to graduate second in his class, without a single demerit.

He came home just in time for his mother's death. Overwhelmed by grief, he found comfort in the company of a distant cousin and great-granddaughter of Martha Washington, Mary Custis. They married a few years later, in 1831, and had seven children. Lee spent the first 17 years of his army career in the Army Corps of Engineers, building bridges, harbors, and docks. He was already 39 years old when he first saw combat—in the Mexican War.

Like Grant, Lee was not at all sure it was a just war. "It is true we have bullied her," he said of Mexico. "For that I am ashamed." But Lee was glad for the opportunity to make a name for himself at last. For 20 months, he distinguished himself in battle: directing a battery of guns at Veracruz; scouting out the enemy position and building a road at Cerro Gordo; and guiding the first assault troops at Chapultepec. "The papers cannot tell you," Lee wrote to his son Custis, "what a terrible sight a field of battle is." For his bravery, the commander of the U.S. Army, General Winfield Scott, promoted Lee to colonel. Scott had no doubt

Mary Custis about the time she married Robert E. Lee.

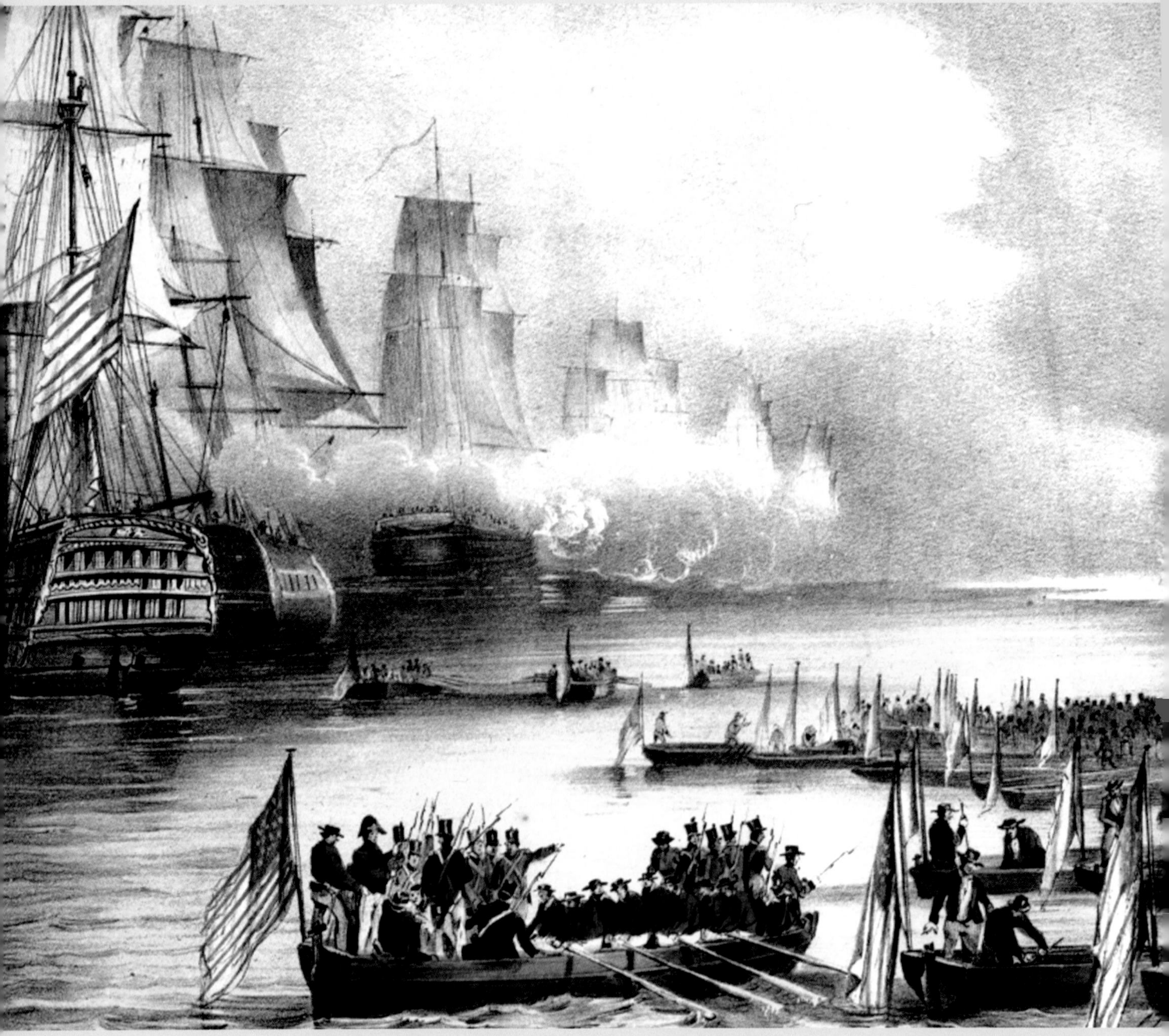

about Lee's military ability. He wrote to a friend, "If the President of the United States would tell me that a great battle was to be fought for the liberty or slavery of the country, and asked my judgment as to the ability of a commander, I would say . . . 'Let it be Robert E. Lee!'"

For a few years after the Mexican War, Lee served as superintendent at West Point. Then, when he got a promotion to lieutenant colonel in 1855, he went out to Texas to take command of a cavalry regiment. He was home on leave on October 16, 1859, when a fanatical abolitionist named John Brown and a band of followers seized control of a Federal arsenal at Harpers Ferry, Virginia. Brown hoped to lead an uprising of armed slaves throughout the state. U.S. Marines under Lee stormed the arsenal and arrested the defenders. Brown was hanged by the state of Virginia a month and a half later.

It was Lee's first skirmish in the conflict that would absorb his life.

Robert E. Lee as he looked at 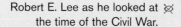 the time of the Civil War.

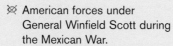 American forces under General Winfield Scott during the Mexican War.

Chapter Two

"Unconditional Surrender" Grant

In 1860, the United States was in turmoil. North and South were arguing about the extension of slavery in the western territories. Many Northerners were outraged by the Kansas-Nebraska Act, which would permit settlers in those territories to decide for themselves whether they would be slave or free. They were even more dismayed by the Dred Scott decision handed down by the Supreme Court in 1857, which stated that no matter where a slave went in the United States, he would remain enslaved. Some argued that this decision, in effect, extended slavery to the free states.

Resolved to block slavery from the territories, some people formed a new political party, the Republican Party. When Republican Abraham Lincoln was elected president in November 1860, Southern states were alarmed. Within two months, South Carolina seceded from the Union. It was followed by 10 other states. The rebellious states formed a new government: the Confederate States of America.

Ulysses S. Grant's father had been a fervid abolitionist from the time Ulysses was a boy. Although Grant's feelings about slavery were not as strong as his father's, he felt no doubt about where he stood on the subject of secession. "I have but one sentiment now," he wrote to his father in April 1861. "That is, we have a Government, and laws, and a flag, and they must all be sustained. There are but two parties now, traitors and

Quick Facts

★ Grant was friends with Simon Bolivar Buckner at West Point, and Buckner had lent him $50 to get home after Grant resigned from the army in 1854. When Grant demanded "unconditional surrender" at Fort Donelson, a disgruntled Buckner wrote back, "The overwhelming force under your command compels me . . . to accept the ungenerous and unchivalrous terms which you propose."

★ At the time, Shiloh was the largest and bloodiest battle ever fought on the North American continent—20,000 were killed or wounded on both sides.

(opposite): The Union assault on Fort Donelson. On February 14, 1862, Union gunboats attacked the fort from the Cumberland River.

Union forces surround Fort Donelson on February 15, 1862.

patriots." Energized for the first time in years, Grant helped recruit Union volunteers in Galena. In August, he was appointed a brigadier general in the U.S. Army. At this time of national emergency, all West Point graduates were in demand. Grant's personal failings were forgotten.

From the day Grant took command of his brigade, things moved quickly. As President Lincoln would discover, Grant was a man of action. "The art of war is simple enough," Grant once said. "Find out where your enemy is. Get at him as soon as you can. Strike him as hard as you can and as often as you can, and keep moving on." In fall 1861, the enemy was fortifying strong points on the network of rivers that fed the West: the Ohio, the Mississippi, the Cumberland, the Tennessee. It would be Grant's mission over the next two years to dislodge the Confederates from their river forts and open the road to the South. When he heard that the rebels were heading toward Paducah, Kentucky, at the juncture of the Tennessee and Ohio Rivers, he rushed troops there first. From then on his army was known as the Army of the Tennessee.

Grant's first important test came in February 1862. His orders were to take Fort Henry on the Tennessee River and then proceed and take Fort Donelson on the Cumberland River. He advanced on Fort Henry with 15,000 men and a squadron of ironclad gunboats under Naval Flag Officer Andrew Foote. The fort fell quickly, giving the Confederate officer in charge just enough time to send most of his men to Fort Donelson.

The contest for Donelson was not so easy. On February 14, Foote's gunboats pounded the fort from the riverside while Grant's troops surrounded the fort on land. The boats themselves were seriously damaged, and Foote was wounded. The next day, while Grant and Foote were conferring on the flagship, the Confederates launched an attack against Grant's infantry. They were about to break through the Union line when the Confederate commander lost heart and ordered them to stop. Rushing back to the front, Grant organized a counterattack that pushed the rebels back to the fort. The next morning, when Confederate general Simon Bolivar Buckner asked to discuss terms of surrender, Grant replied bluntly, "No terms except unconditional and immediate surrender can be accepted." In every newspaper across the country, Grant became known as "Unconditional Surrender" Grant.

Grant had captured an entire Confederate army—15,000 men—and opened up the Tennessee and Cumberland Rivers. A pleased Lincoln promoted him to the rank of major general.

By April, most of Grant's forces were downriver at Pittsburgh Landing, Tennessee, near a little church named Shiloh. Grant was planning his next major attack at Corinth, Mississippi. But on the morning of April 6, General Albert Sidney Johnston led his 40,000 Confederates on a surprise attack of the Union forces at Shiloh. That first day of battle, the raw Union troops were almost wiped out. Nonetheless, when some of his officers suggested they retreat, Grant snapped back, "Retreat? No. I propose to attack at daylight and whip them."

By the time fighting ended after 10 hours the next day, it was the Confederate troops who were in retreat. But the cost of the North's slim victory was shockingly high—more than 10,000 casualties. Some, appalled by the slaughter, demanded Grant's dismissal. But Lincoln said, "I can't spare this man. He fights."

⊠ Union steamboats at Pittsburgh Landing, Tennessee, in April 1862.

⊠ The battlefield at Shiloh.

The city of Vicksburg, Mississippi, before General Grant began his offensive.

Before Shiloh, Grant had thought the war would be over with the next victory. Afterward, he admitted, "I gave up all idea of saving the Union except by complete conquest."

Grant's next big challenge was to take the heavily fortified city of Vicksburg, on the Mississippi River. Its capture would split the Confederacy in two. It took him months in the spring of 1863 to maneuver his troops across the Mississippi and around Vicksburg. First isolating the city, he attempted an all-out assault on May 22. When it was fiercely repelled by rebel defenders, Grant and his troops settled in for a long siege. Union forces dug in and slowly strangled the city. To escape the shelling, Vicksburg residents shoveled caves in the hills and warded off starvation by eating horses, mules, and family pets. Confederate general John C. Pemberton finally surrendered on July 4, 1863. Together with the Union victory at Gettysburg, Pennsylvania, the day before, Vicksburg represented the turning point in the war.

In September 1863, the U.S. Army lost a very costly battle at Chickamauga Creek in northwest Georgia. It looked as if the Union might have to give up Tennessee. Lincoln quickly promoted the one general who always won to the command of the newly created Military Division of the Mississippi. Grant had to defend Chattanooga, Tennessee, an important railroad center and front door to Georgia. On November 25, Grant won the battle of Chattanooga after three days of fighting and opened the way to Atlanta. The Union was taking back the Confederacy, one battle at a time.

Lincoln was overwhelmingly grateful. "I wish to tender you, and all under your command, my more than thanks," he wrote to Grant on December 8. Lincoln had finally found the effective general he was looking for—the one who would win the war for him. The following March, Grant came to Washington, D.C., to receive the highest rank in the U.S. Army: lieutenant general of the Army of the United States. Lincoln looked him over. Five feet eight inches (172 cm) tall and 135 pounds (61 kg), Grant walked with a slouch and blushed whenever anyone used bad language. "He's the quietest little fellow you ever saw," Lincoln wrote a friend.

But beneath his shy manner, Grant was tough and tenacious. One of his officers once said, "He habitually wears an expression as if he had determined to drive his head through a brick wall and was about to do it."

Now this "quietest little fellow" was in command of the U.S. Army. He would be going up against none other than Robert E. Lee himself.

Chapter Three

Marse Robert

When Virginia seceded from the Union in April 1861, Robert E. Lee was offered command of the Union army. He declined. "I have not been able to make up my mind to raise my hand against my relatives, my children, my home," he wrote when he handed in his military resignation. Five days later he became commander in chief of Virginia's military forces.

Lee spent the first year of the war as Confederate president Jefferson Davis's chief of staff. In two months he raised and organized 50 regiments of soldiers and advised Davis on war strategy. In spring 1862, when Union general George McClellan threatened to capture Richmond, the capital of the Confederacy, it was Lee who came up with the plan to stop him. Then, when General Joseph Johnston, the commander of the Confederate Army of Northern Virginia, was wounded in battle, Lee replaced him. Finally he had his own command.

The first thing Lee did was order his flamboyant cavalry commander, J. E. B. "Jeb" Stuart, to find out as much as possible about McClellan's forces. Stuart took off on a daring sweep around the Union

President Lincoln meets with Union general George McClellan. Lee liked to fight the cautious McClellan because he knew what to expect from him.

✖ "Burnside's Bridge" over Antietam Creek, Maryland. During the afternoon of September 17, 1862, Union general Ambrose Burnside made three attacks over this bridge in an attempt to win it. Finally he was driven back.

army, capturing prisoners, seizing supplies, and creating havoc among the Union cavalry. His escapade made him a hero and did wonders for Southern morale.

Now Lee had to eliminate the threat to Richmond. On June 25, he launched what became known as the Seven Days' Battles. For one week—at Oak Grove, Mechanicsville, Gaines's Mill, Savage's Station, Frayser's Farm, and Malvern Hill—Lee attacked the by-now intimidated McClellan. The result was a mixed victory for the Confederates—they lost 20,000 men to the Union's 16,000. But Lee had forced McClellan to retreat back to Washington, D.C. Richmond was safe for another two years.

Lee followed that up with another victory at the Second Battle of Bull Run, or as the Confederates called it, Second Manassas. By now Lee's troops were in bad shape—ragged, hungry, and often barefoot. Lee knew he had to do something decisive to win the war quickly. He would bring the battle to Union-held territory—the border state of Maryland.

On September 5, Lee invaded the North. Eight days later, something amazing happened. On a former Confederate campground, two Union soldiers found a copy of Lee's battle plans wrapped around some cigars. When they were passed along to McClellan, he exulted, "Here is a paper with which if I cannot whip Bobbie Lee, I would be willing to go home!" Still McClellan hesitated, giving Lee enough time to find out about the lost order and get ready to meet the enemy. The armies clashed near Antietam Creek near Sharpsburg, Maryland, on September 17.

It was the bloodiest single day of the war. Union forces bombarded Lee's positions at dawn and attacked the entrenched Confederates relentlessly. A cornfield became a slaughter pen, changing hands several times during the day. Outnumbered almost two to one, the Confederates fought fiercely. "It is beyond all wonder," wrote a Union officer after the battle, "'how such men as the rebel troops can fight on as they do; that, filthy, sick, hungry, and miserable, they should prove such heroes in fight, is past explanation.'"

The rebels fought first of all for the Confederate cause. But they also fought for Robert E. Lee. His devoted soldiers idolized the dignified, gentlemanly Lee, whom they called "Marse [master] Robert." He in turn loved his men. "The rest of us may be descended from monkeys," one veteran said years later. "But it took God to make Marse Robert."

Despite their bravery, the Confederates could not drive the Union army off at Antietam. The next evening, Lee ordered a retreat to Virginia. During the following few months his army rested and retrained. One day his secretary found him sitting on the edge of his camp bed, crying. His favorite daughter, Annie, had just died unexpectedly.

But Lee had no time for private grief. In the next eight months, although outnumbered and outsupplied, Lee had some of his most celebrated victories. The first was at Fredericksburg, Virginia, on December 13. Lee's men were dug into the hills above the city when Union troops under General Ambrose Burnside attacked over open fields. As a Confederate artillery commander said, "A chicken could not live on that field when we open on it." Sure enough, the Union troops were slaughtered. One Federal officer called it "murder, not warfare."

Looking over the bloody battlefield, Lee remarked, "It is well war is so terrible. Otherwise we should grow too fond of it."

Overwhelming though his victory was, it had not destroyed the Union army or its will to fight. Over the winter and spring, the two armies watched each other from either side of the Rappahannock River in northern Virginia and waited for the next battle. It came when the Union army, under yet another new commanding general, Joseph Hooker, crossed the Rappahannock and established itself at Chancellorsville.

✠ Union general Ambrose Burnside. Burnside thought he was unqualified to be commander of the Army of the Potomac. His failure at Fredericksburg certainly proved him correct.

✠ Union general Joseph "Fighting Joe" Hooker proved a disappointment at Chancellorsville. When asked why he had failed, he said, "Well, to tell the truth, I just lost confidence in Joe Hooker."

Quick Facts

★ In 1861, Lee bought a high-strung gray horse named Greenbriar for $200. He renamed him Traveller "because he was such a good traveller." Traveller was Lee's favorite horse.

★ General Thomas J. Jackson received his nickname, "Stonewall," at the First Battle of Bull Run. At one point, when rebel forces were about to give way, an officer rallied them with the words, "There stands Jackson like a stone wall." Lee called Jackson his right-hand man.

★ Civil War battles often have more than one name. Union forces usually named their battles after a physical landmark like a building or a river. Confederates chose the name of a nearby town. This is why the First Battle of Bull Run was called First Manassas in the South and why the Union Battle of Shiloh is also known as the Battle of Pittsburgh Landing.

The skulls of unburied soldiers ✄ killed at Chancellorsville.

To confuse Hooker, master strategist Lee divided his own army, keeping half at Fredericksburg and sending the other half after Hooker's forces. As Union troops began to emerge from an overgrown area of trees and bush called the Wilderness, Confederates under General Stonewall Jackson attacked. Hooker lost his nerve and retreated to Chancellorsville. Then, in a master stroke, Lee ordered Jackson to advance upon the Union right flank. Two hours before sunset on May 2, Jackson attacked, "like a clap of thunderstorm from a cloudless sky," as a Union soldier recalled. The Federals panicked, and over the next two days Lee drove the invaders away.

Everyone agreed that Chancellorsville was Lee's masterpiece. But for Lee himself, it was a dearly bought victory. His trusted friend Stonewall Jackson was dead, mistakenly shot by his own troops. "I do not know how to replace him," Lee somberly wrote to his son Custis.

Flush with victory, Lee decided once again to attempt to defeat the enemy on its own soil. A victory in the North would hurt Northern morale and perhaps force Lincoln to call for a cease-fire and compromise. This time, Lee decided to go into Pennsylvania. The two armies met at a small college town called Gettysburg on July 1 for the three fiercest days of fighting in the whole war. On the first day, Confederate forces had the advantage, pushing the Federals through the town and into a defensive position on the ridges and hills beyond it. The second day ended in a draw. On the third day, Lee decided to send 13,000 men under General George E. Pickett across a mile (1.6 km) of open field to assault the Union line on Cemetery Ridge. It was the worst order he ever gave. Pickett's men were mowed down by a barrage of Union firepower, and the all-important battle was lost. Afterward, Lee admitted, "It's all my fault. I thought my men were invincible."

⊠ Pickett's charge at Gettysburg. The disastrous assault lost the battle for General Lee.

The wounded army limped back toward Virginia to recover. Over the fall and winter, both armies settled down in Virginia again. Then in the spring of 1864 came the news that General Grant had been given command of the whole Union army. Confederate general James Longstreet, who was Julia Grant's cousin, knew Grant well. "That man will fight us every day and every hour till the end of this war," he warned Lee.

And that is precisely what happened.

Chapter Four

The Final Duel

In the spring of 1864, Grant spent his time in Washington, D.C., hammering out a plan with Lincoln. He would stay in the East with the Army of the Potomac and target Robert E. Lee and the 64,000 troops of the Army of Northern Virginia. Meanwhile, his friend William Tecumseh Sherman and his army of 100,000 would press on from Tennessee into Georgia and the heart of the South.

This 1862 photograph of an Army of the Potomac encampment shows the immense size of the army in the field.

Grant readied the army for a long campaign, ordering new troops, new guns, new horses, and new coffins. Lee watched the preparations from the other side of the Rappahannock and made his own plans. When the Army of the Potomac crossed the Rapidan River and headed toward Richmond, he figured that Confederate troops would cut it to bits in the tangled woods of the Wilderness.

On May 4, 1864, the 120,000 men, 274 cannons, 56,000 horses and mules, 835 ambulances, and 43,000 supply wagons of the Army of the Potomac crossed the river on pontoon bridges. The army camped that night on the old Chancellorsville battlefield, strewn with skulls and rusty equipment. Lee attacked at dawn the next day. For two days, the armies fought fiercely, almost blinded by the thick foliage and heavy gunsmoke. Forest fires broke out, turning the battlefield into a hellish inferno and burning many of the wounded alive. Once, a brigadier general galloped up and told Grant that Lee was going to repeat his tactics at Chancellorsville and that all was lost. "I am heartily tired of hearing what Lee is

Union forces crossed rivers on rafts like this one packed with artillery, gunners, and infantry.

Laborers at the Federal supply wharf in Yorktown. The guns, mortars, ammunition, and ships at the wharf demonstrate the vast resources of the North during the war.

Quick Facts

★ On May 6, 1864, at the Battle of the Wilderness, the Confederates were in retreat when General Longstreet's Texas Brigade arrived. "Hurrah for Texas!" Lee shouted. "Charge them!" The Texans surged forward—and Lee, inspired, started to lead the charge himself! "Go back, General Lee!" the Texans immediately shouted, anxious about his safety. In the end, Longstreet himself had to request that Lee go to the rear.

★ At Appomattox, Union and Confederate officers requested permission to visit with old friends from the other side. When General Longstreet arrived at the McLean house to see Grant, Grant shook his hand and said, "Pete, let's have another game of brag to recall the old days." Later Longstreet would say, "Why do men fight who were born to be brothers?"

General Ulysses S. Grant at ⊠ Cold Harbor, June 1864.

going to do," Grant told the brigadier general. "Some of you always seem to think he is suddenly going to turn a double somersault, and land on our rear and on both our flanks at the same time. . . . Try to think what we are going to do ourselves, instead of what Lee is going to do."

There was no clear winner at the Wilderness, and the cost was high: more than 17,000 Union and more than 7,000 Confederate casualties.

⊠ (opposite): Burial party on the battlefield at Cold Harbor.

Rather than leaving the site of battle and retreating to fight another day, Grant advanced south to Spotsylvania Court House. Grant had told Lincoln, "Whatever happens, there will be no turning back." He knew he had numbers on his side. No matter how many men he lost, he could always replace them with fresh troops. Lee could not. With this grim equation in mind, Grant pressed on.

The Battle of Spotsylvania Court House lasted more than a week and involved some of the most desperate fighting in the war. The worst was at a bend in the Confederate trenches called the Bloody Angle. One of Grant's aides remembered it as "probably the most desperate engagement in the history of modern warfare. . . . The opposing flags were in places thrust against each other, and muskets were fired with muzzle against muzzle. Skulls were crushed with clubbed muskets and men stabbed to death with swords and bayonets thrust between the logs in the parapet which separated the combatants." The battle raged on. The Confederates would not yield, and Grant could not break through their line.

The armies paused for breath and, on June 1, raced on toward the next crossroads town, Cold Harbor, only six miles (9.5 km) from Richmond. Here Grant made his worst mistake of the war, sending waves of infantry against Lee's entrenched troops. Within an hour on June 3, 7,000 Union troops were slaughtered. "I have always regretted that this attack was ever made," Grant wrote in his *Personal Memoirs* years later.

In a month of fighting, from Wilderness to Cold Harbor, Grant lost 60,000 men, almost the number in Lee's army. Lee lost 25,000 men. The whole nation, from Maine to Florida, North Carolina to Illinois, went into mourning. In the North, shocked citizens were calling Grant a butcher. But Lincoln stood by his general, praying for a swift victory. Lee still hoped to defeat and demoralize the enemy. "We must destroy this army of Grant's before it gets to the James River," he told one of his

⊠ A 13-inch (330 mm) seacoast mortar, nicknamed "The Dictator."

generals. "If he gets there, it will become a siege, and then it will be a mere question of time."

Lee expected a siege at Richmond and sent troops to cover the capital. But the wily Grant made a wide swing around Lee's troops and crossed the James River to reach Petersburg, a railway center 20 miles (32 km) south of Richmond. If Grant could cut off rail supplies, Richmond would starve. Realizing he had been tricked, Lee rushed troops to Petersburg. The siege, when it happened, was at Petersburg. It would last almost 10 months.

Bogged down in trenches, soldiers on both sides lobbed shells at each other and engaged in sporadic battles. The most infamous, the Battle of the Crater, occurred on July 30, 1864. A Union engineer persuaded General Burnside to dig a tunnel under Confederate defenses and explode a mine, blowing open the rebel line. The explosion did indeed blow a hole 170 feet (52 m) long, 60 feet (18 m) wide, and 30 feet (9 m) deep, killing an entire rebel regiment. What followed afterward, though, was not triumph but tragedy, as one witness wrote: "Everything went wrong. Instead of running around the crater, Union troops charged directly into it. Without ladders, they found it impossible to scale the 30-foot [9 m] dirt walls. . . . Confederate soldiers . . . rushed to the crater's edge and rained a steel blizzard of bullets down on the cornered men." Grant telegraphed to Washington, D.C.: "It was the saddest affair I have witnessed in the war."

By spring of 1865, Grant's troops had cut off the last road from the south into Petersburg and captured the last railway. Lee knew that if he stayed where he was, his army would be completely encircled and its last chance of escape gone. He decided to sacrifice Richmond rather than surrender his army. As long as the Army of Northern Virginia still existed, he reasoned, the Southern cause was not totally lost. On April 2, he telegraphed Jefferson Davis that the Confederate government must leave Richmond. Then he gathered his scattered troops and headed south, hoping to join up with Joseph Johnston's army in North Carolina. But it was hopeless. His exhausted troops could not break through the Union line. On Palm Sunday, April 9, Lee surrendered his army at Appomattox Courthouse.

Grant's terms of surrender were generous. Confederate troops could lay down their arms and go home without fear of being tried for treason, as long as they observed their parole. Artillery and cavalry troops could keep their own mules and horses. "This will have the best possible effect upon the men," Lee said, and "will do much toward conciliating our people." Grant ordered that 25,000 rations be distributed immediately to the starving Confederates. Before leaving, Lee shook hands with all of Grant's staff. When he saw Ely Parker, Grant's military secretary and a Seneca Indian, Lee remarked, "I am glad to see one real American here." Parker responded, "We are all American."

After Grant and Lee exchanged final salutes, Lee rode back slowly through the ranks of his army. Tears filled his eyes as he said goodbye to the loyal soldiers who had fought so hard and sacrificed so much. "Men, I have done my best for you," he said. "Go home now, and if you make as good citizens as you have soldiers . . . I shall always be proud of you." Men threw themselves on the ground and wept. "God bless you, General Lee!" they called out. "Good-bye, Marse Robert."

Twenty years later, Grant described his own mood on that momentous day: "My own feelings, which had been quite jubilant on the receipt of his letter [offering surrender], were sad and depressed. I felt like anything rather than rejoicing at the downfall of a foe who had fought so long and valiantly, and had suffered so much for a cause, though that cause was, I believe, one of the worst for which a people ever fought."

Chapter Five

Let Us Have Peace

President Lee

Robert E. Lee came home to a ruined land. Richmond, where his wife, Mary, was renting a house, was a burned-out shell of the proud city he remembered. His old home in Arlington, now Federal property, had been turned into a national military cemetery. Like every other rebel soldier, Lee had to rebuild his life.

He might have been a hero to the South, but to many Northerners, Lee was a traitor who should be punished. President Andrew Johnson offered amnesty, or pardon, to all rebels who took an oath of loyalty to the United States. But Confederate leaders had to apply individually. In order to regain his citizenship, Lee decided to reapply.

But on June 3, a Federal grand jury indicted Lee for treason. He immediately wrote to Grant, asking him for help. Surely, he said, this did not agree with the terms of surrender he had signed. Annoyed, Grant told President Johnson he would resign from the army if Lee were arrested. The indictment disappeared.

His home and occupation gone, Lee needed a way to make a living. On August 24, he was offered the presidency of Washington College, a

Robert E. Lee

small liberal arts institution in Lexington, Virginia. Lee accepted grate-
fully. The trustees hoped General Lee would attract students; Lee
believed the South needed educated young people to help it rebuild.

At Washington, Lee found peace and a purpose in life. He was an
active administrator, expanding the school curriculum, overseeing a
building program, and attending to each student individually. The

⊠ The Lee Chapel at
Washington and Lee
University, Lexington, Virginia.

electives he introduced included engineering, chemistry, journalism, and photography. Enrollment shot up, and the college became one of the most successful educational institutions of the postwar South.

Lee, however, was not well. The war had worn him out. In late September 1870, he had a stroke and lingered for a few weeks before dying at age 63. In his last hours, he returned once again to his army. "Strike the tent," the old soldier ordered, and then he faded away.

When Lee died, the name of Washington College was changed to Washington and Lee University. Lee's name would be linked to that of his idol, George Washington, forever.

President Grant

Lee lived only five and a half years after Appomattox; the 43-year-old Grant lived another 20. He arrived back in Washington, D.C., on Friday, April 14, 1865. A jubilant President Lincoln asked Grant and his wife to accompany him to the theater that evening. Julia, who did not get along with the difficult Mary Lincoln, persuaded Grant to decline. The next day, Grant, along with the rest of the world, learned that Abraham Lincoln had been assassinated. Julia's dislike of Mary probably saved General Grant's life.

As commander of the U.S. Army, Grant helped get the country back on the road to Reconstruction. He supported the Freedman's Bureau and various Reconstruction acts designed to help newly freed black people. By now the war hero was the most popular man in the country. When the Republicans nominated him as their candidate for president in 1868, Grant couldn't say no. He adopted the campaign slogan "Let us have peace." In his inaugural address, he suggested that his lack of political experience might be an advantage because he didn't owe

✄ A contemporary lithograph celebrates Grant's career, from West Point (bottom left) to Appomattox. Grant ended the Civil War as the most popular man in the country.

Quick Facts

★ In May 1869, Lee received an invitation from the White House and spent a day talking with President Grant. It was the last time the two ever met.

★ Robert E. Lee never received amnesty in his lifetime. His application was found again in the 1970s. In 1975, his citizenship was restored by an act of Congress.

★ When Grant was visiting the Indian maharajah of Jaipur on his round-the-world tour, he was invited to go on a tiger hunt. He politely refused the offer. "Twice in my life I have killed animals," he explained, "and I have regretted both acts ever since."

Grant's Tomb in ✉ New York City.

any political favors: "The office has come to me unsought; I commence its duties untrammeled [uncompromised]."

Unfortunately, Grant's ignorance of politics and government was almost fatal to his presidency. Accustomed to command, Grant was not used to persuading others nor to compromising on his positions. Both are necessary in a government based on consensus and the balance of power. As historian Henry Adams commented, "A great soldier might be a baby politician." Also, Grant's lack of business sense and naive trust in wealthy friends involved his administration in a number of corruption scandals.

To his credit, in 1870 Grant pushed through the 15th Amendment of the Constitution, granting black men the right to vote. He also worked with Congress to pass the Civil Rights Act of 1875, which granted blacks equality in public places and allowed them to serve on juries. Unfortunately, the act was not enforced and was later repealed.

A very ill General Grant writes his memoirs on the porch of his home, June 27, 1885.

When Grant left the presidency after two terms in office, he admitted to friends, "I never wanted to get out of a place as much as I did to get out of the presidency." In 1877, he and Julia went on a triumphant grand tour of the world, meeting the Russian czar, the Japanese emperor, and the queen of England, Queen Victoria. Afterward, the couple settled into a mansion in New York City, where Grant went into a Wall Street brokership—until he discovered that his partner was falsifying the books. Once again a Grant business failed, and he was ruined.

At age 62, Grant was as poverty-stricken as he had been when he was 38, before the Civil War. Not only that, he was in bad health. It turned out that he had throat cancer. He could not die and leave his family destitute. What was he to do?

The answer came from famous author Mark Twain. Grant would write his memoirs, and Twain would publish them and guarantee that

One of the last photos taken of Grant, 1886.

Grant's family would be provided for. In a heroic race against the clock, Grant wrote his *Personal Memoirs* in less than a year, finishing the book in great pain only a week before he died. A masterpiece of American autobiography, *Memoirs* became a runaway best-seller. Two years after publication, Twain was able to give Julia Grant a check for $450,000.

Ulysses and Julia Grant were buried in Grant's Tomb on the shores of the Hudson River in New York City. Inscribed on it are the words "Let Us Have Peace."

Further Reading

Aaseng, Nathan. *Robert E. Lee*. Minneapolis, Minn.: Lerner Publications, 1991.

Archer, Jules. *A House Divided: The Lives of Ulysses S. Grant and Robert E. Lee*. New York: Scholastic, 1995.

Bentley, Bill. *Ulysses S. Grant*. New York: Franklin Watts, 1993.

Clinton, Catherine. *Scholastic Encyclopedia of the Civil War*. New York: Scholastic, 1999.

Commager, Henry Steele. *America's Robert E. Lee*. Lakeville, Conn.: Grey Castle Press, 1991.

Marrin, Albert. *Unconditional Surrender: U.S. Grant and the Civil War*. New York: Atheneum, 1994.

———. *Virginia's General: Robert E. Lee and the Civil War*. New York: Atheneum, 1994.

McPherson, James M. *Fields of Fury: The Civil War*. New York: Atheneum, 2002.

Meyer, Howard N. *Let Us Have Peace: The Life of Ulysses S. Grant*. New York: Collier, 1966.

O'Shei, Tim. *Ulysses S. Grant: Military Leader and President*. New York: Chelsea House, 2001.

Glossary

Abolition—The act of abolishing, or getting rid of, slavery.

Army of Northern Virginia—Confederate army stationed in Northern Virginia.

Army of the Potomac—Union army stationed along the banks of the Potomac River.

Artillery—Weapons, like cannons, that discharge missiles; also the branch of an army armed with artillery.

Bayonet—A steel blade attached to a rifle and used in hand-to-hand combat.

Brigade—A large body of troops made up of two or more regiments and commanded by a brigadier general.

Casualty—A soldier who is killed, wounded, or missing.

Cavalry—The branch of an army that is mounted on horseback.

Confederate—A person who was a citizen of the Confederate States of America.

Confederate States of America—The name of the nation formed by the 11 states that seceded from the United States in 1860 and 1861.

Constitutional Convention (1787)—The meeting of delegates in Philadelphia who wrote a constitution for the United States.

Corps—A tactical unit of the army made up of two or more divisions.

Division—A military unit composed of three to five brigades.

Dred Scott Decision (1857)—A Supreme Court decision that stated that slaves were property even in free states.

Emancipation Proclamation (1863)—President Lincoln's declaration freeing the slaves in the Confederacy.

Freedman's Bureau—The government agency established to help former slaves.

Gettysburg Address (1863)—The speech given by President Lincoln after the Battle of Gettysburg.

Infantry—The branch of an army composed of soldiers who fight on foot.

Militia—An army of citizens with no officially trained soldiers who serve during an emergency.

Musket—A shoulder gun carried by the infantry.

Reconstruction—The period after the Civil War when the former Confederate states were readmitted into the Union.

Regiment—A military unit of about 350 troops, usually commanded by a colonel.

Secede—To withdraw from or leave an organization.

Secessionist—In the Civil War, someone who believed in the right of a state to separate from the United States.

Slavery—The state of one person being owned by another.

Union—During the Civil War, the states that did not secede from the United States of America.

West Point—The academy that prepares officers for the United States Army.

Index